essentia

Responding to Stress

Time-saving books that teach specific skills to busy people, focusing on what really matters; the things that make a difference – the *essentials*. Other books in the series include:

Making Great Presentations

Writing Good Reports

Speaking in Public

Succeeding at Interviews

Solving Problems

Hiring People

Getting Started on the Internet

Writing Great Copy

Making the Best Man's Speech

Feeling Good for No Reason

Making the Most of Your Time

For full details please send for a free copy of the latest catalogue. See back cover for address.

The things that really matter about

Responding to Stress

Dr Tim Rogers & Fiona Graham

ESSENTIALS

Published in 1999 by
How To Books Ltd, 3 Newtec Place,
Magdalen Road, Oxford OX4 1RE, United Kingdom
Tel: (01865) 793806   Fax: (01865) 248780
email: info@howtobooks.co.uk
www.howtobooks.co.uk

British Library Cataloguing in Publication Data.
A catalogue record for this book is available from
the British Library.

Edited by Diana Brueton
Cover design by Shireen Nathoo Design
Produced for How To Books by Deer Park Productions
Typeset by PDQ Typesetting, Newcastle-under-Lyme, Staffordshire
Printed and bound in Great Britain

NOTE: The material contained in this book is set out in good faith for general guidance and no liability can be accepted for loss or expense incurred as a result of relying in particular circumstances on statements made in the book. Laws and regulations are complex and liable to change, and readers should check the current position with the relevant authorities before making personal arrangements.

ESSENTIALS *is an imprint of*
How To Books

Contents

Preface

The world is becoming a more stressful place for many reasons. It is more complex, and the pace of change seems faster. Increasingly we find ourselves taking on roles for which we feel unprepared. Developments in technology which were supposed to make our lives better sometimes just seem to overwhelm us, or else pass us by completely and leave us feeling lost.

There are many ways of responding to stress. The approach we have taken in this book is what we call the Twin Track technique, which combines strategies for making you feel more competent and effective with strategies for allowing you to relax. This dual approach works well because it gets to the heart of what stress is all about. Moreover, and more surprisingly, it leads to interesting and provocative insights about how your life can be more rewarding and fulfilling.

Tim Rogers
Fiona Graham

1 Becoming Stress-Aware

Stress is the feeling of not being able to cope with problems or potential problems in your life.

Nowadays we all hear a lot more of the word 'stress'. Is this because the world is more stressful, or because people are less able to cope, or because the word is being used to mean different things?

In fact, the evidence shows that the world really *is* becoming more stressful. Modern societies are more complex, harder to understand, and more overwhelming. Added to that, few of us are ever taught **how to deal with difficult situations**, or to **recognise symptoms of stress** in ourselves.

But it is also true to say that the word stress is used by different people to mean different things, and sometimes it is misused. Our definition of stress is simple:

Stress is the feeling of not being able to cope with problems or potential problems in your life.

This simple definition is the starting point of being able to **manage stress**.

IS THIS YOU?

• Kate is feeling torn in several directions at once. • Her teenage daughter is having problems at school, her father is suffering from memory problems and poor mobility, her husband is unhappy with his job, and now to cap it all her own boss has asked her to take on extra duties at work. • Kate confides in her best friend: 'I feel I'm having to wear too many hats. I've got to be a mother, a wife, a daughter and an employee. I have to take on a different role in all these situations. I feel I'm juggling with all these different roles and responsibilities and not making a good job of any of them. I lie awake at night trying to think of solutions. Maybe I should give up my job and spend more time with my daughter, but then our income would fall and that would put even more pressure on my husband. My father needs more help and support, and I don't know what to do. I've started snapping at the kids all the time, and getting cross and irritated by the slightest thing. I never seem to enjoy anything these days. I never used to be like this.'

DISTINGUISHING THE TWO COMPONENTS OF STRESS

Take another look at that definition. There is actually more to it than meets the eye. Notice it is about *feeling* unable to cope, rather than *being* unable to cope. This is an important distinction. It means that stress has two components:

- The **situation** you find yourself in.
- Your **response** to that situation.

In this book we will be introducing the concept of the **Twin Track technique**, which is a way of learning how to deal with stress by changing your situation *and* changing your response to your situation. The Twin Track technique is an effective form of stress management for the very good reason that it gets to **the crux of what stress is all about**, and because you learn to apply **your own natural strengths and skills** along two parallel tracks. The Twin Track technique is described in more detail in the next chapter.

Before that, let's have a more detailed look at the two components of stress.

② IDENTIFYING YOUR STRESSORS

In this book we use very few technical terms, only four or five, and we define each of them as we go along. The first of these words is **stressor**. It's an ugly word, but it is useful. Stressors are things which collectively make up stressful situations. In other words, stressors are **things which happen to you**, and which **reinforce your feeling of being unable to cope**. In the example above, Kate has already identified four stressors in her life: her daughter's problems at school, her husband's struggle at work, her father's illness and her employer's expectations. There may be many more stressors in her life that she doesn't realise the significance of, and others of which she is barely aware.

Everybody's life is different, and we all face stressors which are unique and personal. But there are certain common themes which emerge from large studies of stressors:

- Abrupt change.
- Feeling over-committed.
- Feeling under-skilled.
- Joyless striving.

Identifying your stressors means having **a close look at your life** to see which factors are contributing to your stress. Some of these will be obvious, and some will be less obvious. If we take a detailed look at the above four themes you may find that some, or even all, apply to you.

Any kind of change is a potential stressor in your life. The more rapid the change, and the more significant, the greater the resulting stress. Psychologists have actually been able to draw up a hierarchy or 'league table' of stressful events, based on studies of the effect of particular events on the incidence of anxiety and depression. Here are the most stressful types of **abrupt change**:

- getting divorced
- recent illness
- moving house
- bereavement
- changing job
- being made redundant
- pregnancy
- marital reconciliation
- being promoted
- birth of a child.

There are some surprises in this list. Getting back with your spouse, for example, or having a baby or being promoted at work – we would normally think of these as positive events! They are, but even positive events are called stressors if they bring about a **rapid change to the equilibrium in your life**.

The impact of abrupt change has been much studied in recent years. It is not just the speed of the change that is important, or the significance of the change (i.e. how much it affects your life), but also the clustering of events. The effects of these changes are additive – a clustering of four or five events in a year is much more damaging than five events in five years.

That is one of the reasons that Kate is feeling under so much pressure:

'Everything has gone wrong at once. Six months ago we were all fine. I could have coped with these things if they'd been one at a time, but now I feel overwhelmed.'

The second theme to emerge from people who have experienced stress is that they frequently **feel over-committed**. That is certainly true in Kate's case – and she is able to see it herself. Over-commitment is stressful even when it creeps up on you. Here it is not the speed of change which matters but the **complexity**. People experience stress when they find themselves tangled up in more and more complicated networks of commitments and promises and expectations and relationships and arrangements and ... you get the picture. Many of us have experienced this feeling of not being able to see the wood for the trees, and not having the time or skills to unpick the tangled knots which threaten to strangle us.

The more complex our situation becomes, the less able we feel to sort it out, and the more aware we are of our churning stomach and racing pulse.

Feeling under-skilled is similar to feeling over-committed, but here it is a sense of dissatisfaction with one's own inner resources rather than frustration with a complicated life. Sometimes you can feel under-skilled without feeling overwhelmed by outside forces.

Kate later told her friend that what really upset her the most about her situation was not having the skills and expertise to help her daughter. 'I feel I should be able to talk to her, and support her. It makes me feel useless that I don't know what words to use. I always end up saying the wrong thing. I can't be much of a mother if I can't help her through this.'

Feeling under-skilled has a corrosive effect on many aspects of our lives. Our self-belief and self-esteem can be fragile at the best of times, but they can disappear entirely when we start questioning our own skill base. Negative thoughts start creeping in:

'If I can't do this, what can I do? Maybe I'm not much good at anything.'

The final theme to emerge is **joyless striving**. Kate hit the nail on the head when she said, 'I never seem to enjoy anything these days.' Now, you might suppose that this lack of enjoyment could be a *symptom* of stress, and sometimes it is. But for many people, and possibly for Kate, it is more likely to be a *cause* of the stress.

Joyless striving means that life has become a pointless, futile, unrewarding slog. Some people describe this as a sense of **emptiness and loneliness**, others as a **lack of direction and purpose**. The common theme, though, is the absence of a central guiding principle, or organising principle, that gives **meaning to your life** and makes your efforts **rewarding and fulfilling**.

Many people who experience stress say that they feel **disconnected** or **isolated**. They appear to be shouldering the burden of everybody's problems without having a shoulder to lean on themselves. This loneliness might be something obvious, such as a lack of a close confiding relationship, or it might be less obvious and more philosophical, such as a lack of meaning and purpose in life.

One writer described this as feeling 'homeless and a stranger in the world'.

In summary, if you take the time and trouble to try to identify your stressors, you will end up with a clearer picture of your life. This process has to be wide-ranging; you need to look at your job, your relationships, your family, your health, your finances, your friends, and all the inter-connections between them. In short, by the time you've done this, you will understand **the first component of stress: your situation**.

③ IDENTIFYING YOUR SYMPTOMS

The second component of stress is your **response** to the situation. What we mean by this is the **mental and physical reactions** which the stressors provoke. There are many different ways of classifying or sub-classifying the various physical and mental effects of stress, and in this book we will stick with the medical model which in our experience works best. There are other models, and if you prefer alternative explanations that's fine – it doesn't alter the central message of the book.

The first point to make is that the physical and mental effects can be roughly divided into those that you are aware of and those that you aren't. We won't be saying much about those things that are outside awareness, but that isn't because they are unimportant. In fact, they are extremely important, and many of them represent profound chemical changes deep within the body which to some extent *drive* the ill effects of stress. Just for the record, here are the main ones:

- **Brain chemistry**: serotonin, noradrenalin, dopamine.
- **Circulation**: blood pressure, blood supply to vital organs.
- **Hormones**: adrenalin, prolactin, steroids, thyroid.
- **Immune system**: changes to white blood cells and antibodies.

These are the **vital changes to bodily systems** which are **induced by a stressful situation**. In all cases, these changes are destructive to the body rather than protective or helpful. The reason we won't be saying much about them is that we want to concentrate on the effects of which you *are* aware, or of which you can become aware. One of the central points of this book is that **by learning to control systems that you *are* aware of, you can exert control over systems that you *aren't* aware of**.

So, what about the effects that you are aware of? Some of these will be familiar to you already. In keeping with the medical model, we will call these the **symptoms of stress**, and sub-divide them on a medical basis:

- **General**: insomnia, muscular tension, headaches.
- **Heart**: racing pulse, chest pain.
- **Immune system**: infections.
- **Stomach**: loss of appetite, nausea, retching, diarrhoea, heartburn.
- **Skin**: rashes, hair loss.
- **Psychological**: anxiety, panic attacks, depression.

In fact, there is scarcely a system in the body which is unaffected by stress, and there is scarcely a disease known to medical science which is not made worse by stress. The important corollary of this is that **there is hardly a system in the body which is not *protected* by stress management techniques**, and **hardly an illness which is not *improved* by stress management techniques**. If you doubt this, you should get hold of a computer with an internet link and carry out a literature search for stress management using MEDLINE. You will find several hundred papers published in the medical literature in the last five years, establishing beyond doubt the psychological and health benefits of stress management.

MAKING WHAT MATTERS WORK FOR YOU

✓ Spend some time thinking about the pressures in your life at present. If it helps, use a pen and paper to write out a list of stressors.

✓ Make the process as wide-ranging as possible. Include as many aspects of your life as you can think of.

✓ Write out a similar list of all the physical and mental effects caused by the stressors in your life. Be as open as possible. Be prepared to include things that you might not previously have regarded as stress-related.

2 Managing Stress

You have to master two types of technique:
how to feel in control of your stressors,
and how to feel in control of your symptoms.

3

things that
really matter

1 MASTERING THE TWIN TRACK TECHNIQUE

2 USING ACTION TECHNIQUES

3 USING RELAXATION TECHNIQUES

Now that you have learnt how to identify the two components of stress, you are ready to start learning how to **manage** stress. We use the word manage rather than reduce because, as we have seen, the world is a stressful place, and there is no point in pretending that stress can be eradicated or swept under the carpet. Managing stress means **mastering techniques** that make you feel **more in control of your stressors and your symptoms**.

In this chapter we introduce the idea of the Twin Track technique for managing stress. Just as there are two components of stress, there are two components of managing stress. These components can be thought of as **parallel tracks**, and you will learn how to use the two tracks at the same time.

IS THIS YOU?

● Peter is feeling under pressure because more and more of his clients are late in settling their bills. Times are hard for everyone in his line of business, and he knows that most of the late payments are for legitimate reasons. He sympathises with his clients, but nevertheless he needs the money, or else he is going to be in default of his own debts. He is getting anxious, not sleeping at night, feeling sick and losing weight. ● He turns to others for advice. ● 'Relax,' says his wife. 'Ease up a bit. You know they will pay eventually. Don't get yourself in a state about it.'
● 'You've got to get tough,' says his business partner. 'These guys are taking advantage of your good nature. Be more aggressive. Put a bit of pressure on them. Show them you're not a walkover.' ● 'You should try meditation,' says his best friend. 'It worked for me.' ● 'Get more organised,' says his bank manager. 'This is caused by poor planning and poor information management. If you re-organised your office, these things wouldn't happen.'

Relax, get tough, try meditation, get more organised ... The more people he speaks to, the more confused he gets. It's not that any of the advice is wrong, it's just that Peter doesn't have any framework to fit it into. In fact, his confused state is caused by one of the central dilemmas of modern life. Put simply, this dilemma is a conflict between **action** philosophies, which urge you to change your life, and **relaxation** philosophies, which teach you to accept life for what it is.

① MASTERING THE TWIN TRACK TECHNIQUE

As we have seen, stress is the feeling of not being able to cope with problems or potential problems in your life. In order to feel more in control of your stressors and more in control of your symptoms, there are **some things you will have to learn how to change**, and there are **other things you will have to learn how to accept**.

The secret is deciding:

- what things you should change
- and what things you should leave as they are.

In order to make changes, you have to learn how to **take control**, how to be **assertive**, and how to achieve a sense of **self-mastery** and **self-direction**. In order to achieve acceptance, you have to learn how to **relax**, how to **reduce tension**, and how to reach a state of **inner calm**.

Remember, it is not a question of *either/or*. You will need to do both. Your life will continue to be stressful if you simply leave everything the way it is. And it won't be rewarding if you try to change everything, because not everything is changeable. That doesn't mean that you should simply change the things that are easy to change, and passively accept the rest. You need to decide what things to *actively* change and what things to *actively* accept.

You already have most of what it takes to solve problems in your life. What you need is a framework to help you see problems and solutions in a much clearer way.

Quite often we find that people who are feeling under stress get even more stressed when others give them advice. This is because advice which seems on the face of it sensible and well-intentioned is often contradictory and confusing. Each little piece of advice from friends and family clashes with the last piece, leaving the person in the middle feeling hopelessly confused and perplexed.

Action		Relaxation
being assertive		acceptance
taking control	*versus*	equanimity
making changes		calm

What do we mean by the Twin Track technique? Simply this. In order to be able to manage stress, you have to be able to **master action techniques *and* relaxation techniques**.

All of the problems in your life, all of the complex forces pulling you in different directions, can be divided into things which you can change through action, and things which you can live with by relaxation.

This may sound too simple to be true in your complicated life, but in fact it is a powerful technique for cutting through complexity and chaos.

The annoying thing about the problems in your life is that they are always changing. Sometimes they get better, sometimes they get worse, sometimes they are replaced by new ones. But whatever, problems never seem to go away entirely. That's why the Twin Track technique is not a once-in-a-lifetime solution, but a dynamic process that you have to **review and update** regularly.

In fact, some of the difficulties that people run into in life are caused by them using the wrong set of techniques for a given problem. If you have never previously considered your problems in terms of these twin tracks, then you may have been using action techniques to change something which is unchangeable, and relaxation techniques to accept something that you should be changing.

The goal is very simple: **your life should be more rewarding and fulfilling**. Of course, exactly what kind of rewards or fulfilment life will bring varies enormously from one person to the next. What doesn't vary, though, is this:

your goal will be achieved through self-direction and self-control. Not only will you feel more in control of the stressors in your life, but more in control of the symptoms you experience when new stressors come along.

We make a number of key points as we go through the book. **Key point number one** is:

Equip yourself with a set of techniques which you can carry with you wherever you go.

Action and relaxation techniques can be quickly learned, and you then have a set of skills which are with you wherever you go. This adds greatly to your sense of being in control, not only of your familiar surroundings, but of new and unexpected threats.

Let's have a quick look at what we mean by action and relaxation techniques before we go on to describe them in more detail.

② USING ACTION TECHNIQUES

Action philosophies are highly successful in getting you to organise your time and energy. These ideas are often considered to be characteristic of Western thought, and are widely used in business and the corporate world. There is an emphasis on words like 'effectiveness' and 'efficiency', and there is much use of military language: overcome, conquer, master, achieve.

Action philosophies urge you to 'reach beyond your limitations to achieve seemingly impossible goals'. This sounds fine and dandy, but if the obstacles are completely beyond your control you may end up feeling more of a failure than ever.

The problem with action philosophies is that they assume that all the problems in your life can be 'overcome' or 'conquered' in this way. Some problems can be, of course, but other problems are chronic, complex and unchangeable. The more you struggle to banish and defeat these problems, the more useless and hopeless you feel, until finally your situation seems even worse than when you started. We can make a list of the **pros and cons** of action techniques.

Pros

- sense of control
- effective use of time
- applicable at work and home
- allow you to achieve complex or distant goals.

Cons

- lead to obsessiveness and dissatisfaction
- impatience with things that can't be changed
- futile quest for perfection.

We are going to look at action techniques in more detail in Chapter 3, 'Planning your Goals', and Chapter 4, 'Dealing with People'.

Key point number two:

Action techniques allow you to predict and deal with the world around you.

So these techniques work, but they are not enough to help you **make sense of your life**. People who have mastered these techniques are often left with the feeling that something is missing. The most serious charge against action philosophies is that they ultimately reduce your life to a set of *techniques* rather than experiences filled with meaning.

③ USING RELAXATION TECHNIQUES

Relaxation philosophies are often associated with Eastern thought. They teach that happiness and serenity can be reached through a state of inner calm. You don't need to be the master of all you survey, they say. You can achieve fulfilment and reward simply by experiencing life for what it is, and learning to accept the slings and arrows of outrageous fortune.

Pros

- acceptance of your life in the round
- reduction of anxiety
- new kinds of rewards
- a broader view of the world.

Cons

- avoidance of change
- avoidance of decisions
- escapism
- excuse for inertia
- romantic ideal.

We will be looking at relaxation techniques in more detail in Chapter 5, Relaxing, and Chapter 6, Improving Your Sleep.

Again, these techniques work. Your life really *can* be better by learning to love it for what it is and not struggling against the dead hand of fate. Moreover, because these techniques allow you a sense of **self-control** and **self-mastery**, you gain the confidence of knowing that whatever life throws at you, you will be able to **control your inner fears and anxieties**.

Key point number three:

Relaxation techniques allow you to predict and deal with your reaction to the world around you.

But the danger of these philosophies is that you can end up accepting everything that comes your way – good, bad, or indifferent. Acceptance can be a strength, but it can also be a weakness if it becomes **avoidance of change**, the reluctance to take control and say 'I must do something about this'.

At their most pessimistic, relaxation philosophies assume that life is suffering. The purpose of relaxation then becomes the achievement of peace and satisfaction *despite* the pain. While some may find beauty in this idea, the danger is that it becomes an excuse for inertia, passivity and self-denial.

In summary, both of these approaches, action and relaxation, are effective. But neither is sufficient on its own to help you to manage stress. The **most effective stress management technique** comes from realising that **these approaches are not contradictory but complementary**, and you need to **follow them in parallel**.

MAKING WHAT MATTERS WORK FOR YOU

✓ Go back to the list of problems you prepared at the end of the last chapter. Work out which of these problems you might be able to deal with if you had the strength and self-confidence.

✓ Decide which of these problems you would *never* be able to fix, even if you had all the self-confidence in the world.

✓ Work out if there are any problems that you have been trying to change which are basically unchangeable, and if there are any problems that you have been accepting which you should be changing.

3 Planning Your Goals

Plan for the future, because that's where you're
going to spend the rest of your life.
Mark Twain

3

things that
really matter

1 **DISTINGUISHING 'WHAT' GOALS FROM 'WHY'
GOALS**
2 **MANAGING YOUR TIME**
3 **REDUCING THE CLUTTER IN YOUR LIFE**

The first step towards achieving a sense of personal
effectiveness is to work out **what your goals are** and **why**.
This is not as easy as it sounds. A lot of the time, people
who feel under stress will say that they don't know what
their goals are, or that they have too many goals, or that
they don't have enough time to think about their goals!
When pressed further, people will be able to think of one or
two goals, but these are often vague, poorly-focused, or
unachievable. Sometimes people have an unrealistic fantasy
about what life should be like – and they call this their goal.

Whenever someone says that they don't have enough
time to sit down and work out their goals in life – they are
far too busy getting on with things – then you can be sure
that they are storing up problems. Being busy getting on
with things is not always the solution – sometimes it is the
problem. A bit of time and thought spent at this stage can
bring enormous dividends later.

IS THIS YOU?

• *Jenny is feeling frustrated and angry because her two young children have once again damaged some of the new plants in her garden. 'I spend all my time running around after them clearing up their mess,' she says. 'The one thing I have for myself is my garden, and they've ruined it. I don't know why I bother.'* • *She decides to set some goals for herself for the next few weeks, and includes the goal of planning a section of garden for the children to have as their own.* • *Some weeks later, as she sits in the garden relaxing, she watches the children digging in the little plot she has given them. They're making a mess, but it's their mess, and they are happy. She no longer spends hours repairing the damage they've made in her flower-bed.* • *More importantly, she now has a better idea of one of her 'why' goals: why does she want a garden at all? Because it gives her and her children a place where they can enjoy their time together.* • *She reflects on the fact that those few minutes spent on goal planning have not only saved her hours of stress, and changed her garden from a place of frustration to a place of relaxation, but have helped her to look beyond what she wants to do, to why.*

DISTINGUISHING 'WHAT' GOALS FROM 'WHY' GOALS

To start with, let's keep the **goal planning** within a reasonably **short-term perspective**. What are you trying to achieve in your life in the next month? Here is a framework to help you plan your immediate goals.

• **Brainstorm**. Put all your goals down on paper as they occur to you. Write down everything. Do not censor or throw out any ideas at this stage even if they seem silly or difficult.

- **List and prioritise**. Now take all your goals from the brainstorming and prioritise them in order of importance and the amount of difficulty they cause you.

- **Choose a goal** from your list. This does not have to be the most difficult goal but one you feel ready to tackle.

- **List what to do** to achieve the goal. For example who you need to speak to, or what information you need to gather.

- **List any obstacles**, anything that can get in the way of achieving your goal.

- **List how to overcome obstacles**. From your list above, consider how you could prevent or overcome the obstacles you have thought of.

- **Set a plan**. For example, if your goal is a complex one, draw a ladder to help you visualise your selected goal. Put the goal at the top, where you are now at the bottom, and all the steps in between.

- **Review**. Look at how you managed with your goal. Look at what stopped you and how you could overcome this the next time. If you did achieve your goal plan, decide what you wish to do next and go through the same process again.

This probably seems like a lot of writing down – especially if you are not used to planning things this way. Don't worry, you won't always have to write things down this way, but it helps initially because it allows you to organise your thoughts. Writing down goals:

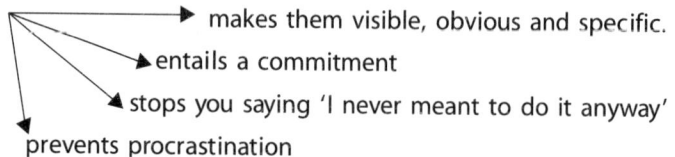

makes them visible, obvious and specific.

entails a commitment

stops you saying 'I never meant to do it anyway'

prevents procrastination

When you see your goals written down, you have a much clearer picture of what is **realistic**, what is **unrealistic**, what you need to **make happen** to achieve your goals, etc. Often, people find that writing things down in this way makes the stressors in their life more comprehensible and more manageable. Things which at one time seemed like a disorganised jumble of stresses and commitments which you carried in your head, now seem like a **short list of achievable targets**.

Most of the goals on your list are probably **'what' goals**. 'What' goals are the things you want to achieve in the next few days or weeks or months; they are your tactical aims. **'Why' goals** are the reasons behind your 'what' goals; they are your lifetime aims. For example, one of your 'what' goals might be, 'Get the kitchen ceiling fixed'. The 'why' goal which lies behind this might be, 'To provide a decent home for my family and myself'.

Key point number four:

Distinguish between 'what' goals and 'why' goals.

Another distinction that is worth making is between **importance** and **urgency**. Some things are urgent (i.e. need to be sorted quickly) but not important (i.e. don't contribute towards your lifetime goals). For example, if your washing machine breaks down and water pours into the kitchen, this is a problem which is urgent but not important. Get it fixed quickly if you can, but don't spend more time on it than on something less urgent but more important, such as relationships within your family. The distinction between 'what' goals and 'why' goals, and between urgency and importance, is vital in goal planning.

Many of the difficulties that people experience in their lives are caused by concentrating too much on the 'what' and ignoring the 'why'.

Sometimes it seems as if modern life, with its rapid pace, forces us to concentrate on the urgent, and ignore the important.

② MANAGING YOUR TIME

The way we spend our time determines the quality of our lives. A large proportion of stress comes from the feeling of not being in control of the sequence of events in our lives. Sometimes we end up feeling so rushed and pressurised that we start to regard time as our enemy, always snapping at our heels, driving us on.

This is an error. From today, **stop thinking of time as your enemy**, and regard it instead as a **precious resource**. Time is one of the most valuable resources, but like all precious resources it has to be properly managed.

Key point number five:

Time is a resource that needs to be managed.

We have already seen that one of the advantages of writing down your goals is that it **avoids procrastination**. This is especially true if you attach **realistic deadlines** to give yourself some guidance and sense of direction. Procrastination is an enormous timewaster. We all know this, but we all do it anyway. You can overcome procrastination by recognising two principles:

- **Procrastination tends to have a common theme.** You probably only procrastinate on certain types of action. These might be anything from social encounters (e.g. speaking to someone) to administrative tasks (e.g.

writing letters), but you should be able to recognise your area of procrastination.

- **Procrastination can be solved by making small changes**. Once you've identified your area of procrastination, you're halfway there. Work out the specific factors that cause you to put things off. Set yourself a target of systematically eliminating these factors. The changes you have to make are much smaller than you think, because your area of procrastination is smaller than you imagine.

③ REDUCING THE CLUTTER IN YOUR LIFE

By now you should have some idea about techniques to plan your goals and manage your time more effectively. Another important aspect of becoming effective in dealing with the world around you is reducing the amount of stuff that clutters up your life.

Some people call this **administrative hygiene**, or **information management**, but another name could be **system management**, and an even better name is **clutter management**. The basic message, **key point number six**, is:

You will have to reduce the clutter in your life.

- **Rule 1: Buy a waste-paper basket.** If you already have one, buy a bigger one. If you can't afford one, use a large black bin-bag. You're going to need something much larger than you think.

'Next to the dog, the wastebasket is man's best friend.' B. C. Forbes

- **Rule 2: Sort out incoming mail within 24 hours.** Do this by sitting next to your huge new bin. Some mail can be chucked out immediately (more than you think). The rest can be put into one of two piles: prompt reply, or wait and see.

- **Rule 3: Touch each piece of paper only twice**. The first touch is to allocate it to the appropriate pile, the second is to deal with it. Don't fall into the trap of shuffling bits of paper round and round. It's very tempting to pick something up, groan with dismay, and put it back. This allows clutter to mount up, adds to your stress levels, and causes missed deadlines.

- **Rule 4: Have a system.** You can devise your own system for dealing with your 'prompt' pile and your 'wait' pile. How prompt is prompt? It depends on your situation. If you run a hectic business, you might have to deal with your prompt pile twice a day – first thing in the morning and mid-afternoon. For domestic things, once a week is enough.

Having a system means having a **regular, time-tabled slot** for dealing with clutter. Decide what is a sensible time for you, and stick with it. Think about this in a positive way: instead of calling it 'time to do bills', which sounds like it is going to make your life *worse*, call it 'clutter management', and remember that it is going to make your life *better*.

A system is not only a way of being efficient and meeting deadlines, it is a great source of stress reduction. For example, if you decide to deal with all your domestic clutter once a week for 30 minutes, you can relax the rest of the time, knowing that all the unpaid bills and other hidden nasties are 'in the system'.

Your system should have one or two simple rules. The prompt pile should be dealt with at your next time-tabled slot. The wait pile should be waiting specifically for other information that you need (for example, to hear from someone else). If you are not waiting for some other piece of information, it should either be on the prompt pile or in the bin. You decide!

We've concentrated here on paper clutter, because most of us are being buried in unnecessary bits of paper. Remember the paperless office? A nice idea while it lasted. In fact, the number of bits of paper circulating around the world is rapidly increasing. The mail service delivers more mail than ever, and most of it is junk.

There are other kinds of clutter, including phone messages, e-mail, faxes, newspapers, magazines, journals and assorted bits of trash. The information revolution was supposed to make our lives better, but just made it more cluttered. In information terms, very little of it is **signal**; most of it is **noise**. Whether we're talking about yesterday's newspaper or this morning's urgent e-mail, the central message of clutter management is just the same: **get rid of it if you can**.

Some people occasionally say that they like having lots of clutter in their lives. They swim in a sea of clutter, and they thrive in it. Good luck to them! If they're happy and fulfilled, they certainly shouldn't change. Most people, though, feel that the trash in their lives is dragging them down.

Remember your 'what' goals and your 'why' goals. If a piece of clutter doesn't fit in with either of these, chuck it in the bin.

The things that surround you should either be useful or beautiful; if they're neither, they're just in your way.

The space that you inhabit, whether at home or at work, should be 'clean', by which we mean **free of the trash that gets in your way**. To achieve purity in clutter management, **concentrate on the signal and eliminate the noise**.

✓

MAKING WHAT MATTERS WORK FOR YOU

✓ Taking into account the list of problems you identified at the end of the last chapter, write out a list of goals for the next week, and a list of goals for the next six months.

✓ Work out your 'why' goals for each of your 'what' goals.

✓ Decide which of your goals are urgent, which are important, which are both, and which are neither!

✓ Define your area of procrastination: what things do you always put off until the last possible minute?

4 Dealing with People

*Be a good listener, but be able to
state your own position clearly.*

4

things that
really matter

Much of the stress in life is caused by our dealings with
other people. This seems obvious enough, and yet how
many of us take the time or trouble to improve our
techniques for handling these situations? It is remarkable
how little attention is paid to this subject, considering that
most of us spend our lives listening, arguing, debating,
haggling, wheedling and negotiating our way through a
complex and confusing world.

The key to having **good people skills** is understanding
what is meant by **being assertive**. It is probably different
from what you imagine. We can emphasise this by
comparing it with two traits that you should *not* possess,
namely submission and aggression.

IS THIS YOU?

• *Richard bought a new computer from a large shop in the high street.* • *He didn't know much about computers but he read the manual carefully, and spent two whole days putting all the components together exactly as instructed.* • *He found that his system kept crashing, and so he phoned the telephone support line (which he'd paid extra for). They had lots of suggestions, but nothing they suggested made any difference. He was advised to phone the hardware manufacturer directly, but when he did he was told that the fault lay with the software. He phoned the software company and was told that the problem lay in the motherboard. He phoned the high street shop to get someone to come out and look at the machine (since he'd paid for on-site maintenance). They told him that their engineers couldn't visit, despite the contract, but they would look at it if he took it back to the shop. He did so, and waited for two hours while they tried to find someone who could look at it. When the engineer finally examined it, he said that there was nothing wrong with the machine, and he advised Richard to take it all home again, try and set it up, and if it didn't work he should phone the software company again.* • *Richard did as he was told, but it still didn't work, and when he phoned the software company they said that it was nothing to do with them. He took it back to the shop, and saw a different engineer, who told him that he shouldn't have brought it in, and that he should take it home and try the telephone support number.* • *At this point, Richard exploded. He shouted at the engineer that he'd already made over 30 calls, he'd taken it backwards and forwards, he was being messed around by everybody, and he demanded his money back. When he slammed his hand on the desk, the engineer called the store detectives and he was evicted from the shop.*

In a situation like this, Richard has been excessively compliant. He has carried out the various instructions that people have given him, and has given no indication to anyone that he is experiencing a rising sense of frustration. We can certainly share his frustration when we see what has happened to him, but it is important to realise that each individual that he deals with along the way has got no idea of the convoluted path that he has already followed. Richard expects people to magically know what has happened already, and he then passively goes along with whatever they suggest. He has not been assertive at any point; he is meek and submissive for 90% of the way, and then finally aggressive at the end. After his loud outburst he is no further forward, and possibly further from a solution than ever.

We will come back to Richard later. What he didn't realise was that in order to achieve his goal of getting his computer to work, there were two things he had to learn about assertiveness:

- **What to say.**
- **How to say it.**

① BECOMING ASSERTIVE

Being assertive involves standing up for your own rights in a way that does not violate someone else's rights. The basic message is: **This is what I think; this is what I feel; this is how I see the situation**.

The message is said without dominating, humiliating or degrading the other person. Assertiveness **involves respect**, not deference. Two types of respect are involved: **self-respect**, and **respect for other people**.

The ability to be assertive depends on making a

fundamental assumption about yourself. This is perhaps the single most important assumption that you have to make in learning how to manage stress. **Key point number seven** states it very simply:

You are just as important as anybody else.

Simple as this sounds, it actually has profound implications for the way you view yourself and others. Being just as important as anyone else implies living in a society of equals. As we will see later, it also means that your relationship with others is based on *interdependence* rather than domination or submission. It certainly does not mean you are more important than anyone else; we are not in the business of promoting arrogance or conceit!

You may be thinking that you already realise you are just as important as anyone else. Perhaps your head knows this, but does your heart believe it? Many people constantly put themselves down, or doubt their own value. Such people *say* that they are just as important as others, but spend most of their lives behaving as if it was not true. Such low self-esteem and low self-confidence lead to an attitude of submission.

- Being submissive involves subordinating your own rights by failing to express yourself. Submission means saying things in such an apologetic, diffident, self-effacing manner that other people can easily disregard you. The basic message is: **I don't count; my feelings don't matter; only yours do**.

- Submission shows a lack of respect for your own needs, and a lack of respect for the other person's ability to take disappointments. The goal is to **appease others** and **avoid conflict**.

Of course, putting other people's needs first is sometimes perfectly appropriate. Not only is it noble and charitable to think of others before yourself, but in an interdependent society it is essential that we all do this from time to time. As we have already said, we are not suggesting that you are the most important person in the universe; we are simply saying that as a basic fact of life **you have to think of your own needs, and what is right for you**.

A lifetime of submission and deference not only spoils your own life, but prevents you from making a full contribution to the lives of others.

It is important to understand the difference between **assertiveness** and **aggression**. Being aggressive involves directly imposing your own view in a way which violates the rights of others. The basic message is: **This is what I want; this is what I feel; what you want is not important**.

The goal is dominating and winning, which is ensured by humiliating, degrading or overpowering other people so that they are unable to defend their rights.

Some of us are always submissive, and some are always aggressive. Many of us, though, switch uneasily between submission and aggression without ever achieving assertiveness. The reason is obvious: our **lack of self-confidence** prevents us from speaking up, and we experience a rising sense of **tension** and **anger** until we finally explode. Having done so, we creep back into our shells, feeling vaguely guilty about having made a scene. Once you **understand the difference between assertiveness, submission and aggression**, you can put that uncomfortable 'switching' behaviour behind you.

② LEARNING WHAT TO SAY

Learning what to say involves **carefully working out your goals** for a given situation. Prepare in advance for a difficult encounter. It might help to write things down. In a situation like Richard's, that means writing down exactly what has happened already, so that you can explain it to the next person you speak to in the chain, and also writing down exactly what you expect them to do. Writing it down helps you to clarify your thoughts, rehearse your argument, and helps you find the right form of words.

Be prepared to repeat yourself. This can be a powerful technique for cutting through someone else's bluster. Don't allow yourself to get dragged into an argument – that just leads to unstable switching between submission and aggression.

Example: Returning defective goods to a store.

You: I'm returning this because it's faulty, and I'd like my money back.

Salesman: Well, in fact... (spurious justification).

You: Yes, but I'm returning it because it's faulty and I'd like my money back.

Salesman: Unfortunately... (irrelevant side-tracking).

You: I'm returning it because it's faulty and I'd like my money back.

Don't worry if this sounds boring or repetitive. As a negotiating tactic it is highly effective. Assertion involves having a clear understanding of your rights, and standing up for them honestly and fairly. You are not there to have an interesting discussion. If you have worked out your basic message, and stated it clearly, you are much more likely to be successful. **Key point number eight**:

Have a clear view of your position, and state it.

③ LEARNING HOW TO SAY IT

Learning how to be assertive also involves an **understanding of non-verbal behaviour**. Non-verbal communication can leak signals revealing low self-confidence or uncertainty. In confident behaviour, non-verbal signals add support, strength and emphasis to what is being said.

Research shows that people who are confident and have good 'people skills' are good listeners. They make a lot of eye contact, are prepared to listen to other people's point of view, but have the courage of their convictions and therefore stick to the point without being distracted or frustrated. If you are worried that being assertive might make you seem 'pushy' or 'selfish', you might be interested to know that these words more often apply to people with low self-confidence, who over-compensate and end up being loud and clumsy in their interactions. Assertive people are **calm**, **confident**, **patient**, and **successful**.

Submissive	Assertive	Aggressive
• Voice		
Sometimes wobbly	Steady and firm	Very firm
Tone may be sing-song or whining	Tone is middle-range, rich and warm	Tone is sarcastic, sometimes cold
Over-soft or over-warm		Hard and sharp
Dull and mono-tonous	Not over-loud or quiet	Strident, shouting
Quiet		Loud
Drops away at end	Steady	Rises at end
• Speech pattern		
Hesitant and filled with pauses	Fluent, few awkward pauses	Fluent

Jerks from fast to slow	Even pace	Abrupt, fast
Frequent throat clearing	Emphasises key words	Emphatic

- **Facial expression**

'Ghost' smiles when expressing anger, or being criticised	Smiles when pleased, frowns when angry, otherwise open	Scowls
Eyebrows raised in anticipation of rebuke	Features steady	Eyebrows raised in amazement/ disbelief
Quick-changing features	Relaxed features	Jaw set firm, chin thrust forward

- **Eye contact**

Evasive, looking down	Firm, but not a stare-down	Tries to stare-down and dominate

- **Body movement**

Hand-wringing	Open hand movements	Finger-pointing, fist thumping
Hunching shoulders	Sits upright and relaxed	Leans forward, arms crossed high
Stepping back	Measured pace	Strides around
Nervous movements	Head held up	Head thrust forward

- **Behaviour**

Hope you get what want	Ask for what you want	Try to get what you want
Rely on others to magically know what you want	Ask directly, openly and confidently	Choose any tactic that works
Feel hurt/a victim.	Have respect for yourself and those around you.	Threaten and manipulate people to get your way.

④ UNDERSTANDING BARRIERS TO ASSERTIVENESS

If the difference between assertiveness, submission and aggression now seems pretty clear, you may wonder why people don't find it easy to be assertive. The reason is that there are several barriers to assertiveness:

- **Being unclear**: You may not have decided what you really want in a particular situation. Remember your goal planning. Work out your 'what' goals and your 'why' goals.

- **Self-doubt**: You may undervalue yourself, and feel that you do not have the right to stand firm and make demands. You may have been brought up to think this, or it may be the view of other people in your life.

- **Poor presentation**: Perhaps you fear anger or negative responses, and come over as vague or uncertain. This is caused by lack of practice. Keep going! You will be surprised how effective you can be once you have mastered the techniques of assertiveness.

IS THIS YOU?

- *Richard returned to the shop the next day with his friend Jack, who was a skilled negotiator.*
- *Before they left home Jack made a detailed note of all the calls Richard had made, and all the suggestions he had been given.* • *At the shop, Jack asked to see the manager and then waited patiently while the manager finished with another customer.* • *When the manager appeared, Jack carefully and calmly explained the entire situation. Richard noticed that Jack addressed the manager by his name, made lots of eye contact, was cool and unruffled.* • *He listened carefully to the manager's interruptions, but always returned to the main point, which he had already worked out. 'The point is this,' he said. 'The computer was bought from this shop, and doesn't work properly. None of us knows whether the problem is to do with the hardware or software or anything else, but that doesn't really come into it. You supplied him with defective goods. He is returning it to you and you either have to give him a replacement or refund his money.'* • *The conversation took many twists and turns, but Jack always came back to this, his central goal.* • *They left the shop an hour later with a brand new system, fully checked out and operational.*

MAKING WHAT MATTERS WORK FOR YOU

✓ Go back to the list you prepared at the end of the last chapter.

✓ This has gradually evolved from a list of pressures in your life, to a list of problems you want to tackle, to a set of goals you have defined.

✓ Now that you can be assertive, decide whether you want to adapt your list of goals. Are there problems that you didn't include in your list because you felt you didn't have the ability to change things?

✓ Work out the barriers to assertiveness which prevent you from making changes in your life.

5 Relaxing

It is not your situation that causes you most
trouble, but your response to your situation.

4

things that
really matter

1 **USING YOUR BODY TO RELAX**

2 **USING YOUR IMAGINATION**

3 **USING YOUR SENSES**

4 **USING YOUR SITUATION**

As we have seen, it is possible to make positive changes in your life. By having a clearer picture of what your **goals** are, and a clearer sense of **self-worth**, you can take control of your life and start removing those obstacles to fulfilment.

However, this is only half the story. Even when you are successful in making changes in your life, you may not feel fulfilled. The constant quest for change, for control, for improvements, even for perfection, can become a neurotic ideal. It leads to obsessional behaviour, dissatisfaction, and ultimately despair. Perfectionism always leads to unhappiness, if it is applied to every aspect of your life.

The world isn't perfect, and never will be. Your life isn't perfect, and it is irrational to expect it to be. Some things, in fact, are unpleasant but cannot be changed. And if it is impossible to do anything about a particular problem, the only rational thing to do is to learn how to live with it.

IS THIS YOU?

• Laura was 15 years old when she was diagnosed as suffering from diabetes. • To start with she wasn't that bothered, but after a year she got fed up with the constant monitoring of her glucose, and she objected to having to inject herself with insulin, not because it was sore but because it made her different from all her friends. • She started missing out the occasional injection, and didn't turn up for her appointment at the hospital. She got angry with her mother every time her mother reminded her about her insulin. She dreamed about running away from home, not having to bother about injections and blood tests and hospital appointments. • The one thing that she still really enjoyed was swimming, and she decided to train even harder, and to stop her insulin, and to prove to the world that she wasn't diabetic. • Over the next two weeks she became much weaker, until she could hardly train at all. • Her physiotherapist gave her a relaxation tape to reduce the pain in her legs. She used the tape every morning and every evening, and felt more relaxed than she'd been in months. Her sleep improved too. • Finally, one morning she woke up and realised that she'd been running away from her diabetes, trying to pretend that it wasn't there, or trying to change it when it wasn't changeable. She made up her mind that since the diabetes wasn't going to go away, she would have to learn to live with it. • She started her insulin again, and her health improved rapidly, and within six months she was winning medals again at the swimming club.

Key point number nine:

If it is impossible to do anything about the situation, the only rational thing is to accept it.

How is it possible to **accept the unacceptable**? By learning to view your life from alternative standpoints. The first step towards acceptance is **relaxation**. Learning how to relax can be life-changing, not for the superficial reason that by relaxing you 'calm down', but for the deeper reason that **relaxation techniques allow you to view your life in an altered light**.

You may not realise it, but you already have the essential ingredients to become an expert in relaxation techniques. You are using all of these ingredients right now! They can be combined in interesting and complex ways to produce powerful results.

What are the essential ingredients? **Your brain, your body**, and **your senses**. Let's take a look at some of the interesting combinations.

⓵ USING YOUR BODY TO RELAX

Let's start with some of the simplest techniques – exercises designed to **reduce muscular tension**.

Some people seem to think that this approach can't possibly work for them, because their body is not the cause of the problem. This is to misunderstand the powerful nature of relaxation exercises. Your body is not the *cause* of your problems, of course, but it is a **symptom carrier**. Stress causes your body to enter a state called autonomic arousal, in which your nervous system is in a heightened state of tension.

Autonomic arousal causes many of the symptoms of stress that you will already be familiar with (insomnia, raised pulse, fretfulness etc.), along with one or two features that you will be less familiar with. One of the most important and least recognised symptoms of stress is **muscular tension**.

Muscular tension is a state of raised muscle tone in

various muscle groups throughout the body. This causes aches and pains, headaches, tiredness, fatigue, etc. These symptoms feel so *physical* that they are often mistaken for symptoms of physical illness rather than stress. They make you feel worse, and add to your malaise.

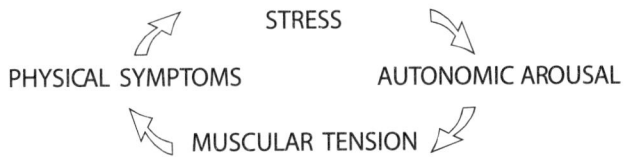

STRESS

PHYSICAL SYMPTOMS   AUTONOMIC AROUSAL

MUSCULAR TENSION

One of the basic principles of relaxation is that you learn to use **systems which you *can* control to alter those you cannot**. As an example, you cannot directly control your heart rate, or the amount of perspiration produced by your skin, but by learning some simple exercises you can reduce the level of arousal in your nervous system, which in turn allows you to feel calmer, to have a slower pulse rate, and to stop your palms from sweating.

Key point number ten:

Learn to use systems which you can control to alter those you cannot.

Progressive Muscular Relaxation was developed in the early years of the 20th century by an American doctor called Edmund Jacobson. His theory was that anxiety and deep muscular relaxation cannot co-exist, so if you abolish one you abolish the other. Today, Progressive Muscular Relaxation (PMR) is one of the most widely used relaxation techniques in clinical practice. Dr Jacobson's theory has since been brought up to date by modern neurophysiology, and the treatment gradually refined.

The technique is best done at a time when you can find privacy and quiet. Most people choose to do the exercises in the evening, usually in the bedroom where they can get some peace. The ideal way, in fact, is to use an audio-cassette tape which specifically has the PMR exercises, but if you can't get hold of a tape, go through the following routine.

1. Lie on your back and get as comfortable as possible.

2. Starting with your feet, gently stretch and then release one muscle group at a time. For example, flex your foot to the ceiling for a few seconds, then away from you for a few seconds, then release.

3. Feel how the tension flows away from the muscles in your foot when you release the stretch.

4. Keep going with the stretch and release, gradually moving from your feet to other muscle groups in the following order: legs, buttocks, pelvis, stomach, back, shoulders, chest, arms, hands, neck, face.

5. Do one leg at a time, and one arm at a time, and learn to recognise the feeling of relaxation.

6. The whole cycle of exercises should take about 20 minutes, and needs to be repeated once a day. You will find that within a few days you will be able to recognise muscular tension, and will be much more able to control it.

Regular PMR exercises in the evening will improve the quality of your sleep, which allows you to wake up feeling more relaxed, which gives you more energy and enthusiasm to face the day.

Learn to distinguish **muscle tone** from **muscle tension**. Tension is a sign of autonomic arousal, as we have already discussed, while muscle tone is firmness in the muscle caused by fitness and strength.

There are some techniques which increase **muscle tone** while **reducing muscle tension**.

- Being alert to your **posture** is one of the simplest techniques. A slumped posture contributes to poor muscle tone, making you feel flabby and weak. The more you slump, the more strain is placed on other systems of your body, and the more aches and pains you will feel. Learning how to improve your posture improves the muscle tone in your back and abdomen and shoulders, so that your body feels *firm* without feeling *tense*.

- Using a **stress ball** is another useful and quick technique. The ball is usually made of rubber or plastic, and is very pliable and easy to squeeze. Not only does it involve the stress/release cycle in a similar way to PMR, it helps develop muscle tone in your hand and arm, making you feel stronger and healthier.

- Tension in the **jaw muscles** is another common symptom of autonomic arousal. It leads to teeth-clenching, facial pain, neck pain, headaches etc. It can be eased by simply stretching the jaw muscles slowly, as if yawning, and repeating this two or three times.

Perhaps there are some **sports** or **exercises** that you do already, and that you find relaxing. If so, keep going! Relaxation techniques don't have to be some special tricks that you learn – they can be very much part of your normal life.

Walking is one of the most healthy and therapeutic activities, for lots of reasons. Swimming, cycling, golf – whatever sport you do, it's likely to be an effective part of your relaxation routine if you approach it in the right frame of mind.

You often hear people saying that they like sport

because 'it gets me out of myself'. This is very accurate. Concentrating on a particular physical skill, such as a difficult putt on the golf course, involves clearing your mind of all kinds of distractions and, just for a moment, stepping out of your worries.

② USING YOUR IMAGINATION

The human imagination is one of the most complex and powerful tools available. It is a magic carpet, and it can take you **out of your current situation** to somewhere **calmer** and **more relaxed**.

Visualisation is one way of doing this. We all know what it's like to day-dream. We usually assume that it's not healthy, or that it's a waste of time. We may even have been shouted at for indulging ourselves. But our dreams are a vital part of who we are. They are the well-spring of our creativity, and we can draw on them for strength and comfort.

We don't want to suggest that you idle your time away by dreaming dreams and seeing visions. But the ability to dream means the ability to visualise, and that is a skill which you must cherish and improve.

At their simplest, visualisation techniques are used to **form pictures in your mind**. These can be combined with other approaches (for example, some of the exercises discussed above).

Visualisation is like an internal cinema – one which you take with you wherever you go.

Once you have got the hang of the PMR exercises, try combining them with some visualisation techniques. Here are some examples of the kind of **mental images** that people are able to conjure up as part of a relaxation technique:

- Lying on a beach in the warm sun, with the waves lapping near your feet.

- Lying in a grassy meadow, with a river babbling nearby.

- Sitting on a hilltop surveying the fields and valleys below.

Take your time with these visualisation techniques. To start with, to make it easier, try the visualisation immediately *after* you have completed the PMR.

When you picture yourself in the scene, don't just think of how it looks. It's more important to imagine how it *feels*. Imagine the feel of the sand, the warmth of the sun, the sound of the waves – step inside the scene, and live it.

The ability to visualise is something that **improves with practice**. Flexing your imagination in this way has all kinds of unexpected spin-offs – which we'll come to later.

Another simple and useful technique which is related to visualisation is 'framing'. This is the ability to **create a mental picture of something that scares you**, or something that you feel threatens to overwhelm you.

- First of all, allow **a clear picture of the threat** to form in your mind. The scarier and more threatening it is, the better. This image can be of anything: your boss, your enemy, your bank manager. It doesn't have to be a person or an object – it can be a feared event such as your redundancy or financial ruination.

- Once the mental image is very clear and threatening, gradually **shrink it down in size**, and imagine it as a small picture in a frame. Again, flex your imagination. Don't let the mental image be vague or poorly-focused – make it very specific and very real. Visualise the exact size of the picture, the exact colour and texture of the frame. Experiment with your mental image – you can make it bigger or smaller at will.

You might be thinking, 'what's the point in that?' Try it, and you'll see. The point is to be able to **control the extent and severity of your stressors**, not by changing the threats themselves, but by changing your view of them.

This type of technique gives you an ability which is of great significance in your life – the freedom to step out of your situation.

No matter where you are, and what you are doing; no matter how intolerable the pressures put upon you; no matter how unpleasant and yet unchangeable the situation, you are always able to play out a rich pageant in this secret theatre of the mind.

Another, and more complex, way of using your imagination is by learning to **experience time in a different way**. Most of us, when we are worrying about a problem, are so consumed by the problem that we are unaware of the **immediacy of the moment**. It is possible to rise above this.

A curious thing about anxiety is that it is almost exclusively concerned with 'what if's' and 'if only's'. In other words, worries about what might happen, and regrets about what did happen. **Apprehension about the future, and guilt about the past**. It's fairly obvious that the first casualty in this is **the present**.

Loss of the present is literally a 'waste of time'. All that any of us are ever capable of experiencing is the present moment, but a lot of the time it washes past us in a haze of apprehension or regret. All the 'nows' pass away, and once gone can never be recaptured.

Learn to experience the immediacy of the moment. This improves with practice. It is another change in viewpoint, and one you can learn to control. **Key point number eleven**:

Experience the immediacy of the moment.

We have briefly touched on three techniques of the imagination. All of them require an effort, but with practice **the effort becomes less and the rewards greater**. Don't think that you can't do it, because as a child you did it all the time! Children are experts of the imagination, while adults forget or become rusty.

Like the physical techniques we have discussed already, these techniques also bring about an altered state physiologically, by reducing autonomic arousal. Just as importantly, as we have seen, your imagination allows you to **step out of your situation** and to **step out of yourself**.

③ USING YOUR SENSES

All the information you have ever taken in about the world, you took in through your senses. Your senses have been biologically tuned over millions of years to be hypersensitive to particular stimuli. One of the reasons that people today can feel stressed-out is that they bombard their sensory nervous system with stimuli that signal threat or danger.

Loud noise, rapid movement, raised voices, sudden change – all the things we take for granted and accept as 'normal', our senses perceive as potential warning signs. The nervous system puts itself into a state of readiness for **fight or flight** – and that's what we mean by autonomic arousal.

By understanding this, we can sometimes find out **what our bodies are trying to tell us**. It's not that our bodies are wanting zero stimulation – far from it. The nervous system thrives on stimulation, and we thrive in environments which are complex, varied and stimulating.

But just as some kinds of sensory inputs can *increase*

autonomic arousal, some can *decrease* it, and help us to relax. This may seem like common sense, but it also happens to be a scientific fact, and one which is important for reducing stress.

Many of the things you do already to relax are various kinds of sensory stimulation. This is what comes naturally, because it feels right. But sometimes it helps to think ahead, to **pre-empt stress by seeking out those soothing stimuli** when you don't even feel you need them. Remember, relaxation is a state of altered physiology – one that **you can learn to control**.

What will be soothing for one person might be boring or unpleasant for another. The only way to have an effective relaxation technique is to know what kinds of things *you* find soothing. Think about what this might mean for *you*.

- **Seeing**. What things do you like to look at? For some people it's a beautiful painting, for others a sunset, and for some a city skyline. But it doesn't have to be an object or a landscape; it could be your children, or even your car! The point we're making is that your vision is a powerful way of relaxing. It comes so naturally that some people feel that it isn't a 'proper' relaxation technique, but that argument is completely upside down. The 'proper' relaxation techniques are the ones that evolution has equipped us with over millions of years, and this is one of them.

- **Hearing**. What things do you like to listen to? Again, it doesn't have to be the obvious things, like your favourite music, although that might be part of it. All kinds of other things that you may hear have a soothing effect, and it helps to be able to tease out the pleasant noises from the unpleasant and tiresome hubbub. For some people it will be birdsong, and for others the noise of the traffic on the road outside the bedroom. Whatever, it's up to you. But give it some thought.

- **Smell**. What things do you like to smell? Again, it's an individual thing. It doesn't have to be orange blossom or lavender. There is no magic about this. It's pure biology. Some smells are pleasant because they remind us of our childhood, when we were safe and comfortable. Some smells (like fruit) are pleasant because nature has made them that way to increase the chance they will get eaten!

- **Touch**. Touch is associated with all kinds of powerful signals. It's not just about touching, but about being touched. Massage is an effective relaxation technique, and there are a number of ancient arts such as shiatsu that are making a comeback. Some of these techniques come with a fair dollop of hocus-pocus.

Massage works well, but it's pure biology. It's soothing because of the direct tactile stimulation of your skin and connective tissue and muscles and nerves. Moreover, it's doubly soothing because it's being done by somebody *else*. We have evolved as social animals, and creatures who touch each other, but touch is forbidden within our modern social setting.

④ USING YOUR SITUATION

So far, this book has been largely about **self-direction** and **self-control.** These are two guiding forces that help to shape your life. We have been emphasising that you can take responsibility for sorting out some of the problems in your life, and take responsibility for making sense out of your life.

We do not want to give the impression that the goal is independence. Many people seem to believe that independence is a useful endpoint, but in our view that is a mistake. As we have said already, **it is interdependence that we are aiming for**, not isolation and detachment.

We mention this now, because one of the **powerful sources of relaxation** in your life will be found **in your relationships**. Relationships may not be necessary for functioning, but they are necessary for *healthy* functioning. **Key point number twelve**:

Relationships are the vitamins of your mental health.

Again, this may seem so obvious that it hardly needs to be stated. Often, though, it is things which are obvious which *do* need to be stated, because they are so easily overlooked. When you are troubled you instinctively turn to your trusted confidants: your partner, your family, your friends. It is so instinctive that it doesn't seem to be a proper 'relaxation technique', but for all the reasons that we have already covered, it is natural, and proper, and right.

Encouraging and fostering **mutually supportive relationships** is what healthy functioning is all about. That is what we mean by interdependence. The closest and most intimate relationships confer the greatest added strength.

Interdependence also implies the ability to put yourself into another's position. Other people share their problems with *you*, which is not only helpful to them, but which adds to the breadth of your experience by allowing you to enter the world-view of someone else. Over time, and across a network of diverse relationships, we build a picture of life (and our own situation) which is **richer and deeper** than our own narrow experience would give us.

True interdependence allows you to forget yourself for a

while. To be able to live through another, or with another, is a privilege, and one that allows us to achieve **acceptance of unresolved problems** in our own lives. In fact, many of the techniques that are truly effective for relaxation work on the principle of learning to 'forget yourself'. We have looked at a few of these techniques: physical exercises, techniques of the imagination, sensual experiences, and healthy relationships.

Key point number thirteen:

Forget yourself, at times.

It is also important to learn to live with question marks. Not all of the puzzles in life will be answered. Some of your mental compartments will be left tantalisingly open, and some business that you would like to finish will be left unfinished.

The risk of relaxation techniques is not that they don't work, but that they might work too well. In that case, the danger is that you drift into a state of apathy, or a twilight world of escapism, where nothing really matters. If you are too eager to achieve acceptance of everything, you lose the motivation to make the changes that are necessary in your life. Just as **the danger of action is perfectionism**, the futile pursuit of a neurotic ideal, so **the danger of relaxation is escapism**, replacing reality with a romantic ideal. For your life to be rewarding and fulfilling, you need to draw these ideas together into a **workable strategy**.

MAKING WHAT MATTERS WORK FOR YOU

✓ What relaxation techniques do you use already? Try to think of as many as possible, using the headings from this chapter.

✓ Which ones work best? Are there some that don't work at all?

✓ Make a list of four new relaxation techniques, one from each section of the book.

✓ Try each of these out, starting today.

6 Improving Your Sleep

Disturbed sleep is sometimes the first symptom of stress, and often it is the hardest thing to put right again.

It's a bit of a cliché to say that we spend a third of our lives asleep – but it also happens to be a fact. The amount of sleep our bodies need varies enormously from one individual to another, and it varies at different times of our lives. There is a gradual decline in the amount of sleep we need to function properly, but most of us will have times in our lives when we feel we are not getting as much sleep as we need.

We have included this chapter here because **a disturbed sleep pattern is often the first sign of stress**. The tricky thing about sleep, though, is that the more you chase it, the more elusive it becomes. As soon as you get to the stage where you are positively *trying* to get some sleep, you have already lost the battle. Sleep is something that is so complex, and yet so natural, that it cannot be captured in this way. It is possible to **get back to a good sleep pattern**, but only by attending to the three basic areas described here.

IS THIS YOU?

• Alison was always a good sleeper until she had to resit her second year exams at college. The anxiety of the resit, plus the late nights studying, disrupted her sleep, and for several weeks she was tossing and turning at nights and feeling lousy in the morning. • What surprised her was that even when she passed her resit, and didn't have any particular worries or stresses, her sleep just wouldn't return to normal. By this time, she was really enjoying herself during the day, with no exams to worry about. She varied her getting-up time, according to how well she'd slept the night before, and depending on what lectures she had. Sometimes she would be up at 8, but sometimes 11 and occasionally not until 1 in the afternoon. • She didn't let it disrupt her life. She still did plenty of partying, and managed to keep herself going with coffee and alcohol. Sometimes she wouldn't get to bed until 3 or 4 in the morning, although on other days she felt so exhausted that she would crash out at 8 or 9 in the evening. • She found that it helped if she could cat-nap during the day (it helped the partying anyway). Her flatmate liked watching soaps on TV at about 6 or 7 in the evening, and Alison could be guaranteed at least an hour snoozing in front of the TV then.

You may think that Alison's case is extreme, but it's actually pretty common. Even if your routine is not as off-the-wall as that, it's worth considering why her sleep is still badly affected. After all, if she is so busy going to lectures and parties, you might expect her to be so tired that she would sleep like a log.

① HAVING A ROUTINE

Sleep is a biological process. It is a reflection of one of the fundamental **biological rhythms** which govern the inner working of our bodies. 'So what's new?' you might be thinking. The point about biological rhythms is that they are complex and delicate, and **if we mess around with them they start misbehaving**. There are all kinds of hormonal, chemical and metabolic changes which take place in our body in a 24-hour cycle, and these rhythms are kept in synchrony by an important time-keeper, which is **routine**.

In fact, tiredness does not guarantee sleep. If your routine is smashed to pieces, you won't sleep no matter how tired you are. The reason is that your body doesn't know whether you are about to get up, about to go to bed, or about to have a cat-nap. Those delicate and sensitive rhythms which fine-tune every aspect of your metabolism will be rendered chaotic if your body does not have a reliable routine. Why is cat-napping so destructive to a good sleep pattern? Not for the obvious reason that your body gets a little bit of sleep and therefore 'isn't tired', but for the much more important reason that cat-napping disrupts the 24-hour sleep-wake cycle, so that your body chemistry starts firing up again, ready for another 16 hours of action.

If we're sounding like party-poopers, it isn't all bad news. If you want to go out and party all night sometimes, fine. All it means is that you should go to bed at roughly the same time of evening *normally*, and get up at the same time each morning *usually*.

Key point number fourteen:

Have a routine, and stick to it.

② WATCHING WHAT YOU EAT AND DRINK

You may have noticed that Alison was making some obvious mistakes with regard to caffeine and alcohol. In fact, **what we eat and drink has a major impact on how well we**

sleep. Coffee is an obvious example because caffeine is a powerful stimulant; real coffee contains much more caffeine than instant coffee, but strong tea can be another potent source of caffeine and other stimulants. Many people who have experienced sleep problems find that their sleep returns to normal once they give up tea or coffee after about 6 or 7 in the evening.

Alcohol is another big source of sleep problems. We all know that alcohol can make us sleepy, and therefore we sometimes think that it will 'give us a good night's sleep'. In fact, alcohol is more likely to cause you to wake up during the night, or to toss and turn all night, or to cause 'early morning wakening' where you lie in bed from 4 or 5 in the morning until it's time to get up.

Eating a large meal late in the evening is another mistake; it might make you feel drowsy, but it will also make you feel bloated and uncomfortable. But if you don't have anything to eat, you will be restless and agitated. Hunger is one of the 'wakeup' calls that the body uses to establish its own rhythms. One of the best ways of promoting sleep is to have a light snack of carbohydrate-rich food just before you go to bed. Milk is useful for this; hot milky drinks are even better. Things like toast or biscuits also have the same effect. Carbohydrates stimulate the body to produce insulin, which has a sleep-inducing effect. It is a natural narcotic; it worked well for you when you were a child, and it works well now.

Key point number fifteen.

Have a light snack at bed-time, but no tea or coffee.

③ CHANGING YOUR SLEEP ENVIRONMENT

The final piece of the jigsaw is your sleep environment. This doesn't just mean your bed or bedroom, although they are obviously important. Sleep will come more easily if you are **in a place where you can feel relaxed, and safe and comfortable**. If there is something awful about your bedroom, such as noisy neighbours on the other side of the bedroom wall, you may have to give serious consideration to moving to another part of the house, or changing your bedroom in some way to minimise the noise. This can sometimes be done fairly easily by moving key pieces of furniture.

A fresh start can be very therapeutic for sleep problems. Changing the bed to another part of the room, changing the ambience of the room, or making one or two subtle changes to your sleep environment can make a huge difference, especially if you have had sleep problems for months, and have started dreading going to bed.

Your sleep environment should be a place of refuge, somewhere that you look forward to going to, and not a place that becomes associated with 'problems'.

Finally, the sense of being active and effective during the day, and sleeping well at night, are what stress management is all about. If you are using the action techniques discussed in Chapters 3 and 4, and you are addressing and resolving your stressors during the day, you should be able to use your relaxation techniques in the evening. There is no need to lie in bed worrying about your life, when you have already worked out a set of goals and plans to put into action during the day. Tell yourself that you are going to bed to relax, rather than going to bed to sleep. **If your goal is relaxation, sleep will come naturally**. In fact, you will sleep much better if you say to yourself, 'It doesn't matter if I sleep or not. The main thing is I am comfortable and relaxed.'

MAKING WHAT MATTERS WORK FOR YOU

✓ Establish a routine to allow your sleep-wake cycle to be restored.

✓ Work out if caffeine or alcohol contribute towards your sleep problems.

✓ Change your room around, or make more subtle changes to your room, to give yourself a fresh start.

✓ Make sure that your sleep environment is a place where you feel comfortable.

✓ Tell yourself that you are going to bed to relax. Allow sleep to come naturally.

7 Doing and Being

Each individual is not a carbon copy cut from social pressures and norms, but is unique, singular, and irreplaceable, and thus significant.
Viktor Frankl

So far, we have made it clear that you have to run a dividing line down the list of techniques you need for managing stress. You have to use **action techniques for making changes** in your life, and **relaxation techniques for reducing** the symptoms you experience. We have deliberately kept these separate, and emphasised the distinction. Most people find it helpful to separate things in this way: it gives them a clearer idea of **what they want to achieve**.

In this final section we are going to go one step beyond that. Once you have completely mastered the technique of **dividing** or **separating** problems in this way, you are ready for the next step of drawing these things **back together** into a seamless whole.

① INCREASING SELF-EFFICACY

Self-efficacy is a type of self-belief. It is the belief that you can carry out a particular task to achieve a particular consequence. People who have self-efficacy have:

- confidence in their own abilities
- a good grasp of their strengths and weaknesses
- the knowledge that they are just as important as anyone else
- and the ability to devise and execute a plan of action.

Self-efficacy is one of the main sources of resilience, because if your self-belief and self-confidence are strong enough, you persevere towards your goal whatever the obstacles and setbacks. The **greater your self-efficacy**, the less **vulnerable you are to anxiety and stress**, especially in the face of threatening events. People with low self-efficacy, by contrast, do not feel confident that they can achieve their goals, and therefore they give up in the face of minor setbacks. This makes them much more vulnerable to stress and anxiety.

The most powerful way of increasing self-efficacy is by trying things out for yourself, but it is also influenced by sources of information derived from learning (e.g. reading a book) or by talking to others. All of the techniques described in Chapters 3 and 4 are designed to improve your self-efficacy.

If you can plan your goals, organise your time, reduce your clutter, and achieve assertiveness, your self-confidence and self-belief will grow.

Every interaction you have with another person is a potential learning experience. People need other people to achieve the full development of their potential. You gain self-efficacy by **continual participation** in a world of things and events, and always in encounters or dialogue with other people.

② SELF-TRANSCENDENCE

Self-transcendence is a type of freedom – the freedom to reach out and make a connection with something other than yourself. It is an ancient idea, and one that forms a large part of some Eastern philosophies such as Taoism. The term transcend (literally 'to climb over or beyond') describes what every human is capable of achieving at every moment of his life. We can rise above the past, rise above our immediate situation, transcend ourselves.

The ability to 'climb beyond' ourselves can lead to **new insights of our situation**. Kierkegaard used the term 'Augenblick', meaning the 'blinking of an eye'. This is the moment when a person suddenly grasps the meaning of an important event in the past or future. The new meaning brings about a **new orientation** of the person towards the world; **consciousness is expanded**, and **the world looks different**.

Self-transcendence sounds very fancy. It sounds like the kind of thing that mystics and holy-men achieve after years of training. It doesn't have to be anything quite so profound. We are not talking about plunging into the depths of the 'oceanic feeling' – just dabbling at the shallow end.

Bending down at night to kiss your sleeping child – that is exactly the kind of experience that can lead to a sense of calm, to a different view of yourself and your world. Gazing at a painting, listening to music, watching a sunset – each of these can be powerful enough for the effect we are describing here. Each of these can take you out of yourself, albeit briefly. Sure, there are deeper kinds of experience: people who meditate say that it helps them to find some kind of spiritual enlightenment. Good luck to them! But that isn't necessary.

There is a spectrum of self-transcendence. At the light end, you can find relaxation and tranquillity. At the other end, some people claim to have found something more significant. For the purposes of what we are describing here, the light end is preferable. It is not to do with the search for the 'meaning of life', but with the freedom to step out of yourself, and to **take a broader and larger view of your life**.

The techniques discussed in Chapter 5 are designed to help you achieve a state of relaxation. They are not supposed to be heavy or intense. If you are able to find techniques that work for you, and you use them regularly, you will find that over time they will help you achieve an altered view of yourself and your life.

③ TWO HALVES OF A WHOLE

The techniques we have described, for action and relaxation, are more than simply problem-solving techniques, although it is quite useful to think of them in that way. At a deeper level, they are reflections of two quite distinct aspects of your life: **doing** and **being**.

- **Doing** refers to all the acts and tasks and processes that make up your life. Looking after your family, running a household, helping your friends, holding down a job; all of the things which require you to take responsibility and make decisions. If you have high self-efficacy you will feel successful in all these things. You will feel that you are back in the driving seat.

- **Being** refers to your awareness of your existence. Full awareness involves the knowledge that you are unique, and that you have more freedom than you think. Being implies acceptance of your life in the round. Although this is a hard idea to explain, most people have an intuitive idea of what it means. It is not about what you do, or how successful you are; it is about *who* you are.

Doing and being are both vital aspects of your life. To ask which is more important is like asking which contributes more to the area of a field, the length or the breadth. Doing is concerned with means and ends – what you want to achieve, and how, and why. It is a view of the world based on 'instrumental significance' – in other words, how useful the things around us will be to help us achieve our goals. Being is less concerned with striving, and less obsessed with means and ends.

The reason we use the term Twin Track technique is to emphasise that action and relaxation techniques are not opposite poles, as they might appear. They are parallel processes, **reflections of doing and being**. You have to be able to **use both tracks**, and to constantly shift and adjust the relative weight and importance of each. The problems in your life will be constantly changing. The likely threats to you and your family will be different today from a year ago, and may be different again a year from now. Your abilities and strengths will fluctuate, and so will your vulnerabilities.

To live your life in this way means to give yourself the best chance of developing your potential.

The beauty of stress management is that what starts as a simple process, to reduce the pressures in your life, leads to a deeper view of what your life is all about.

At the start of the book we said that our goal was to help you feel able to cope with problems in your life. That was our 'what' goal, and this is our 'why' goal: because you are a unique individual, and you can play a full part in an interdependent society.